Habit Chains: 7 Steps to Build Powerful Habits that Stick (in 5 Minutes or Less)

By Dominic Mann

Table of Contents

Habit Chains: 7 Steps to Build Powerful Habits that Stick (in 5 Minutes or Less)

    Table of Contents

    Preface

        The Habit Problem

        Mini Habits

        Hack Your Habits

    Habit Chains: A Brief Introduction

        Habits Shape Your Life

    Your Brain on Habit Chains

        Down the Snow Hill

        You're a Zombie

        You're a Slave

    The BIG 5 of Habit Chains

        The BIG 5

    How to Build a Habit Chain

        Simple Disciplines

        How to Create a Goal-Oriented Habit

        How to Build a Habit Chain (with Examples)

Supercharge Your Mornings

- Lead the Pack
- Habit Linking
- Habit Linking Examples
- Supercharge Your Morning Routine with Habit Chains
- Start Each Day with a Powerful Habit Chain
- Taking Action: Creating a Powerful Morning Habit Chain
- Create a Morning Habit Chain that Lifts You to Greatness

Habit Chains and Decisions

- Habit Chain Decision Automation

Mix & Match

- Habits to Supercharge Your Productivity
- Habits to Supercharge Your Health
- Habits to Supercharge Your Career
- Habits to Supercharge Your Happiness

Habit Chain Tips

- Habit Chain Tip #1: Keep It Short and Snappy

Habit Chain Tip #2: Make the Chain Easy to Grip

Habit Chain Tip #3: Linking and Sandwiching

Habit Chain Tip #4: Chain by Category

Habit Chain Tip #5: Don't Break the Chain

Conclusion

Preface

The Habit Problem

"A small daily task, if it be really daily, will beat the labours of a spasmodic Hercules."
– Anthony Trollope

We all have things we want to do.

For some, it's to get in shape. For others, it's to have a successful career. And for others yet, it's to win the local pigeon racing competition.

The only question is, how do we do these things?

Fortunately, the answer is surprisingly simple. The way to get what you want is to take consistent action toward a specific goal.

To lose weight, consistently eat healthy. To have a successful career, consistently be of value to your customers and company. To win the local pigeon race, well, I'm not exactly sure of that one—but you can be sure it requires consistent action.

We all know what we need to do. But, for some reason, most of us don't do it.

You see, habit is the key to consistent action. But there's a problem: Habits are *hard*.

They take an *average* of 66 days to form—often longer. This means that most people struggle with habit formation and, more often than not, fail.

This is a problem—a problem that this book aims to solve.

Mini Hopes

If habit formation is so hard, why hasn't somebody already come up with a solution?

Well, quite a few self-help gurus have actually attempted to crack the habit code. The only problem is that they're going about it all wrong.

A popular example of this is the book *Mini Habits* by Stephen Guise. It's a great book, but it is based on the idea that the way to make habit formation easier is to make habits that are, well, "mini."

The logic behind this, Guise says, is, "big intentions are worthless if they don't bring results ... doing a little bit is infinitely bigger and better than doing nothing."

In the same vein, the blogger James Clear advises his readers to follow what he calls "the two-minute rule." This rule stipulates that a new habit should take no longer than two minutes to execute, else you're likely to abandon it altogether.

While these tips *do* help, they don't get to the bottom of the problem. It's like telling yourself that because it's hard to earn a million dollars a year, you're going to lower your goal to $30,000 a year—it doesn't solve the fundamental problem.

Hack Your Habits

"Your net worth to the world is usually determined by what remains after your bad habits are subtracted from your good ones."
— *Benjamin Franklin*

This book aims to solve this problem by taking a

completely different approach—one that exploits the inner-workings of the human brain. It empowers you to build *more* habits, build habits that actually *stick*, and—most importantly—build all these habits with *less effort.*

This new approach is called *habit chains*. It's a unique habit formation process that lets you hack into your brain's circuitry and install new habits with ease. Even better, you can use the power of habit chains to enhance all areas of your life, supercharging your productivity, health, wealth, and happiness.

Habits Chains: A Brief Introduction

habit chain

noun

    1. a sequence of habits.

    "he created a habit chain to improve his health"

    "complex activities can be made easier with habit chains"

A habit chain is a series of connected habits. For example, you might brew your morning coffee, meditate for a few minutes, and then write down the day's three most important tasks.

By linking habits together, you get to create numerous habits with virtually no additional effort—just as holding a single iron ring requires no more effort than holding a chain of iron rings. Put simply, it's like getting five (or more!) habits for the price of one.

In addition to allowing you to create *more* habits, habits chains also make habit formation *easier*.

By linking new habits to old habits, you eliminate much of the effort typically associated with habit formation.

It can be difficult, for example, to make a habit of doing 10 pushups every day. That's 66 days—more, in some cases—of exercising the self-discipline to not skip your new habit for "just today." It's no wonder most people fail to form new habits. Even after weeks of dedication, it can still be a struggle to cement a habit once and for all.

But, do you know what's far easier to do? It's far easier to make a habit of doing 10 pushups before your morning shower. Building new habits by taking advantage of old ones makes everything easier.

Finally, in addition to enabling you to build *more* habits with *less effort*, linking habits together makes it all that much easier for you new habits to *stick*. For example, you're much more likely to stick to the goal of

For example, imagine you want to develop a gratitude habit. Which of the following two habits do you think will be more likely to stick:

1. Every day, say one thing I'm grateful for.
2. Before I take my first bite of breakfast, say one thing I'm grateful for.

Of course, the second habit is many times more likely to stick. Why? Because it's linked to another habit.

And then, if you so desired, you could add another habit: After breakfast, spend five minutes journaling. You could then add another habit: Read five pages of an inspirational biography. And so on.

Before you know it, you have an incredibly powerful habit chain. And because these habits are linked together, they're *easy* to form, they'll *stick*, and you can create *more* of them.

SUMMARY: *A habit chain is a sequence of habits. By linking habits together, a habit chain lets you build more habits, build them with less effort, and have them stick.*

Habits Shape Your Life

"Mastering others is strength. Mastering yourself is true power."
– Lao Tzu

The ancient Greek philosopher Aristotle once wrote, "We are what we repeatedly do. Excellence, then, is not an act, but a habit."

In other words, **you are your habits**. Or as U.S. founding father and man-on-the-hundred-dollar-bill Benjamin Franklin said, "Your net worth to the world is usually determined by what remains after your bad habits are subtracted from your good ones."

Obviously, habits can have a profound impact on your life. Habits can either make you or break you. They can either lift you up or drag you down. Either way, you're the one that decides. Do you build yourself up with good habits or let yourself be consumed by your bad habits?

Because new habits can be so difficult to form, the decision isn't quite so clear cut for more people.

But, as you probably guessed, habit chains completely change this. By building *more* habits that *stick* with *less effort*, habit chains let you harness—and amplify—the power that habit has to shape your life.

SUMMARY: *You are your habits. Habit chains give you a whole new level of control over your habits. Therefore, habit chains empower you to shape your life.*

Your Brain on Habit Chains

A Brain of Connections

"*Our brains contain one hundred billion nerve cells (neurons). Each neuron makes links with ten thousand other neurons to form an incredible three dimensional grid. This grid therefore contains a thousand trillion connections—that's 1,000,000,000,000,000 (a quadrillion). It's hard to imagine this, so let's visualise each connection as a disc that's 1mm thick. Stack up the quadrillion discs on top of each other and they will reach the sun (which is ninety-three million miles from the earth) and back, three times over.*"

– Nessa Carey, The Epigenetics Revolution

The human brain is the most complex structure in the universe. That's right—that jelly-like thing between your ears.

In order to work quickly and efficiently, the brain has evolved to find a perfect balance between overwhelming complexity and a rapid accessibility of information. After all, you don't want to contemplating the millions of memories, connections and ideas in your brain when confronted with a sabertooth tiger.

So how has the brain overcome this dilemma?

Here's how: The human brain links concepts together.

That's why we end up with stereotypes of Asians being great at maths, African-Americans loving deep-fried chicken, and muslims being terrorists. While such stereotypes don't serve us very well in modern society, it certainly helped our distant ancestors associate sabertooth tigers with danger and buffalos with a full belly. It's just how the brain works.

However, there's more to this than there at first seems. You see, the brain is *built* to function like this, and so it creates equally compelling connections in other areas of our lives. For example, we've all had an old song on the radio trigger a flood of past emotions.

Our brain is built on links and connections. We can't see the entire contents of our brains at once, but if we think (or do) one thing, our brain supplies us with related concepts, memories, and ideas.

The brain is nothing more than a collection of connections.

But what does all this have to do with habit chains?

Here's what: Habit chains let you use the brain's natural tendency to link things together to your advantage.

Down the Snow Hill

"Any act often repeated soon forms a habit; and habit allowed, steady gains in strength, At first it may be but as a spider's web, easily broken through, but if not resisted it soon binds us with chains of steel."
— Tryon Edwards

The brain relies on connections and links (whether legitimate or not) for the sake of efficiency. It's much easier to just assume that all sabertooth tigers are dangerous than it is to do an in-depth risk analysis whenever encountered by one.

A great example of the brain's propensity to create connections is Pavlov's dogs. The crux of the story is that after ringing a loud bell whenever feeding his dogs, the psychologist Ivan Pavlov noticed that his dogs started to salivate whenever they heard the bell—regardless of whether or not any food was actually being served.

This phenomenon is encapsulated more succinctly by the phrase, "neurons that fire together, wire together." In the case of Pavlov's dogs, their brains subconsciously learned to associate the ringing of the bell with food.

In his book on neuroplasticity, *The Brain That Changes Itself,* Norman Doidge explores an excellent analogy for this phenomenon:

"As Pascual-Leone's metaphor illustrates, neuroplasticity is like pliable snow on a hill. When we go down the hill on a sled, we can be flexible because we have the option of taking different paths through the soft snow each time. But should we choose the same path the second time or the third time, tracks will start to develop, and soon we will get stuck in a rut—our route will now be quite rigid as neural circuits, once established, tend to become self-sustaining."

What all of this demonstrates is not only the potent role that habitual behavior plays in our lives, but also just how intrinsic habits are in our lives and in the way our brain functions. As the ancient Greek philosopher Aristotle said, "we are what we repeatedly do."

We are literally creatures of habit. It's in our biology!

As we cannot avoid our brain's snow-hill-like characteristics, the only question is this: Where do we want our sled to end up? After all, we obviously don't want our sled to end up in a semi-frozen lake or a smelly gutter!

By cultivating positive habits, we can control where our metaphorical sled ends up.

You're a Zombie

"The conscious mind may be compared to a fountain playing in the sun and falling back into the great subterranean pool of subconscious from which it rises."
– Sigmund Freud

You're a pilot locked out of the cockpit. The plane is just going along on autopilot, executing pre-programmed instructions. Like a zombie.

Unless we grab a crowbar, bust open the cockpit door, and make a deliberate effort to seize the aircraft's controls, we go through everyday life on autopilot. It's the default setting. We just go through the motions, execute well-trodden habits, and live as a zombie.

In fact, studies have found that over 40 percent of our actions each day are habit. Not decisions. Not deliberate behaviors. Just habit—us stuck in our own tracks on the snow hill.

More shocking is the fact that it's estimated that between 95 to 99 percent of everything we do is controlled by the subconscious. Even decisions that we *think* we make—such as whether or not to pick up an object—show up in the subconscious before reaching the conscious mind.

While the conscious mind processes information at about 40 bits per second, the subconscious mind performs at 40 *million* bits per second. That's right. The subconscious—our "zombie" brain—is a *million* times more powerful than our conscious mind.

If that doesn't convince you of the potency of habit, I don't know what will. Habit is the key that allows us to access the mighty subconscious.

That leaves us with the following question: How can you harness the immense power of habit?

The path to actualizing this awesome force begins with the following realization...

<u>You're a Slave</u>

"Chains of habit are too light to be felt until they are too heavy to be broken."

— *Warren Buffett*

You're a slave. Your master is habit.

Fortunately, you can choose who your master is. You can choose a tyrannical sadist who has made it their life's work to bring you misery, or you can choose a far kinder master who works to bring you long-term happiness and desires to set you free with an abundance of riches.

The choice seems like a no-brainer, right? So why is it that most people choose (yes, choose—inaction is a choice) to stay with the worse of the two masters?

Here's why: The bad master is the default choice. That's where everybody starts. And guess what? It's damn hard to escape. Even harder is the journey to the good master.

In *The Greatest Salesman in the World*, Og Mandino says the following:

"In truth, the only difference between those who have failed and those who have succeeded lies in the difference of their habits. Good habits are the key to all success. Bad habits are the unlocked door to failure. Thus, the first law I will obey, which precedeth all others is—I will form good habits and become their slave."

If you must be a slave to habit, be a slave to good habits—and habit chains are a highly effective way to fill your life with an abundance of good habits.

It's simple. First, determine the actions you need to consistently take in order to reach your goal. Second, build a habit chain that automates these actions. Third, become a slave to these habits.

And just like that, you can use habit chains to fast-track

your progress toward your biggest goals.

The BIG 5 of Habit Chains

Your brain is nothing more than a collection of connections. Fortunately, you can exploit this by using habit chains to become the sculptor of your life.

Our brain naturally links everything together. It creates stories where their are none (also known as the narrative fallacy) and is all too eager to create stereotypes.

It also links habits together.

We've all gotten out of bed one morning, gone to the toilet, taken a shower, brushed our teeth, and brewed a cup of coffee—all before we've even fully woken up or consciously decided to do anything.

You've probably more than once found yourself standing in the kitchen in sheer amazement (or horror?). You'd gone through the entire morning without so much as a single thought, as if a robot were controlling your body. This is both good and bad.

The bad: This type of morning routine is—at best—an incredibly impotent habit chain.

The good: You can exploit the brain's behavior and use this same natural tendency to create powerful habit chains with life-changing results.

Now, it's time to meet the *BIG 5* of habit chains.

<u>The BIG 5</u>

You might still be a little skeptical about the whole idea

behind habit chains. After all, they can't really be *that* effective, can they?

Here are the five driving forces that make habit chains so damn effective:

1. Automation: The brain automates regular behavior. As such, the right habit chains can propel you toward your goals on autopilot.

2. Linking: The brain loves things that are linked to something else (it also usually forgets things that aren't related to anything). Habit chains work by linking habits together. This makes building new habits virtually effortless.

3. Order: The brain is built for consistency. Habit chains exploit this need for consistency.

4. Mind: The brain learns to associate everything with a specific state of mind (remember: old songs on the radio and

Pavlov's dogs). By creating powerful habit chains, you train the brain to enter a high-performance state of mind at specific times (also known as "the zone", "flow", or just "work mode").

5. Momentum: Having lots of small wins throughout the day builds momentum. Habit chains build waves of momentum that carry through the day and lead to high productivity. This kind of momentum also gets Newton's first law of motion working in your favor: "Objects in motion stay in motion."

The BIG 5 makes one thing clear: If you want to put most complex structure in the universe (read: your brain) to work and direct it toward your goals, habit chains are the way to go.

How to Build a Habit Chain

Simple Disciplines

In his book *The Slight Edge*, Jeff Olson vigorously preaches the importance of the little things. He reminds us that success isn't the result of a lucky break or any single action. Rather, success is the result of all those little decisions we make.

Should I watch TV or hit the gym?

Should I sleep in or get up and work on that business idea?

Should I drink that can of soft drink or grab a glass of

water?

Olson explains, "Simple disciplines repeated over time will create success, while simple mistakes repeated over time will create failure."

Luckily for you, habit chains make these "simple disciplines" all that much easier to make a part of your life.

How to Create a Goal-Oriented Habit

Here's how to create a goal-oriented habit:

1. Determine the action necessary for success.
2. Link this action to an existing daily habit.
3. Execute the habit daily.

Easy as one, two, three.

Here's an example for a wannabe novelist:

1. Decide to write for 30 minutes every day.

2. Link your writing habit to your shower habit.

3. Write for 30 minutes every day after taking a shower.

Of course, you could also link this new habit to dinner and write for 30 minutes every evening after dinner.

How to Build a Habit Chain (with Examples)

You can then link on another habit (to the aforementioned writing habit). And then another. And another. That's how habit chains work.

For example, someone who wants to do some freelancing on the side might start with the following simple habit chain:

1. Wake up.

2. Make a cup of coffee.

3. Spend 20 minutes browsing freelance job postings and messaging potential clients.

4. Take a shower.

5. Spend 40 minutes working on client projects.

6. Have breakfast and head to day job.

By sandwiching new habits between existing habits, you eliminate much of the struggle that usually accompanies habit formation.

Someone who wants to become their company's most valuable employee might start with the following habit chain:

1. Journal. Find three positives and three negatives regarding the previous day's performance. Determine how to improve.

2. Prioritize and plan the day. Write down three MITs (Most Important Tasks) that need to get done.

3. Take morning shower (or have breakfast).

Then, in the evening:

4. Dinner.

5. Spend 30 minutes becoming an industry expert—read and learn.

6. Brainstorm 10 ideas for providing more value to customers, improving the company, and improving the industry.

Or, if you want to keep things short and snappy:

1. Identify three ways to improve and become an indispensable employee (five minutes).

2. Outline the day's top priority—the MIT (five minutes).

3. Read five pages of an industry-related book (five minutes).

4. Brainstorm three ways to provide customers more value or otherwise improve the industry in general (five minutes).

That's it. Four habits, 20 minutes, and well on your way to becoming an indispensable employee. You could then link this potent habit chain onto an existing habit—such as breakfast—to make it all that much easier.

Supercharge Your Mornings

Lead the Pack

When I was in school, I used to compete in cross country running races. One of the greatest determinants of your finishing place (i.e. first, second, third, etc.) was how you started the race during the first 20 seconds.

If you managed to get out in front of the crowd at the very start, you almost always finished very well. If you started poorly and remained in the middle of pack at the beginning of the race, you almost always finished poorly.

The start is everything—and not just for long-distance

running races.

It's true of first impressions when meeting people. It's true of people judging books by their covers. And it's true of everything else—including and especially the way you start your day.

Most people start their days reactively. Snooze buttons, spilled coffee, "zombie-mode", traffic jams, and stress are all part of the average person's morning routine. Not exactly empowering, to say the least.

The ultra-successful and ultra-productive, however, start their days proactively. Like cross country champions, they get out in front early.

Early rising, exercising, journaling, daily goal setting, and personal empowerment are all part of the high-performers morning routine. They start their days powerfully and build lasting momentum.

Mornings tend to be best because of an evening we too often find ourselves depleted of willpower and mental stamina. After a big day of work, it's far too easy to just slip on the couch and avoid the work required to make progress toward our goals.

In the morning, however, we are fresh. We have an abundant supply of willpower and energy, making it the perfect time to work toward our goals. As a side note, this is why you see the ultra-successful exercise of a morning—rarely of an evening.

Now, let's take a look at how you can use habit chains to maximize your mornings.

Habit Linking

If you're like most people, you have a pretty disempowering morning routine. So the question is this: How can you go about creating a powerful morning routine?

The ordinary approach to building new habits is difficult and thus unlikely to deliver the results you desire. Fortunately, by looking at your morning routine from a habit chain perspective, it's easy to see that there is a much easier approach: Link new habits to old ones.

Here's a few examples.

Habit Linking Examples

Daily Planning Habit: After brewing my morning coffee, I will write the three most important things I need to get done today.

Meditation Habit: After planning my day (above), I will meditate for one minute.

Walking Habit: After meditating (above), I will take a

five minute walk around the block.

Pushup Habit: Before I take my morning shower, I will do a dozen pushups.

Reading Habit: Before I go to sleep, I will read five pages of an empowering book.

Gratitude Habit: Before I turn the car on to drive to work, I will think of one thing I am grateful for.

Any of these could, of course, be mixed up. You could think of something you're grateful for in the shower. You could listen to audiobooks while commuting. And so on.

By examining your life from a habit chain perspective, it becomes all that much easier to link on empowering new habits and, more importantly, be sure that they'll stick!

Supercharge Your Morning Routine with Habit Chains

How can you use the power of habit chains to supercharge your morning routine?

Start off simple. Most of us already have some sort of existing morning routine—no matter how clumsy. Some sort of chain of little habits such as coffee, shower, breakfast, and all that.

The simplest way to get started creating a more empowering morning routine is to start off by linking one small habit onto your existing morning habit chain.

I'll use an example from my own life to demonstrate this point.

For a long time, I'd been meaning to eventually get around to making a habit of brainstorming ten ideas every day. And yes, I mean a *long* time. I'd been meaning to do this for months.

Recently, however, I've finally made it a part of my morning routine.

How?

Each morning, immediately upon waking, I go downstairs and brew myself a cup of coffee. In the past, I would just chuck the coffee into a thermos and drink it while taking a cold shower.

Finally committing to forming this habit, I decided to exploit my habit chain theory. I simply sandwiched this new habit between two existing links in the habit chain that made up my morning routine: Brewing coffee and showering.

So ask yourself the following two questions:

1. What empowering habits would you like to start your day with?

2. What existing habit can you link it to?

And just like that, you can supercharge your morning routine.

Start Each Day with a Powerful Habit Chain

I believe that there are three components essential to an ultra-powerful morning routine. These elements help build momentum and catapult you into a day of extreme productivity:

- Intense exercise.
- Daily planning (could also be referred to as journaling or daily goal setting).
- Inspiration (such as by listening to an empowering audiobook or podcast, or reading the biographies of history's greats).

How can you add these potent ingredients to your

morning habit chain and supercharge your mornings?

Taking Action: Creating a Powerful Morning Habit Chain

As advised earlier, start off simple. Start by adding only one new habit to your morning habit chain—and an easy one at that. I would suggest daily planning.

To make it easier, link it to an existing habit. Likewise, you could "sandwich" it between two existing habits.

For example, you could commit to spending five minutes planning your day (or determining the single most important thing you need to get done that day—a daily goal) after brewing your morning coffee.

After several days of executing your modified habit chain each morning, add an additional habit "ring" to the chain. For example, after setting the resolution of the day (i.e. daily planning), read ten pages of the biography (or autobiography) of someone you greatly admire—be it Napoleon, Steve Jobs, Sam Walton, or anyone else.

Alternatively, you could link in this new habit "ring" to another part of your habit chain—such as by listening to an audiobook while commuting to work.

Finally, after executing your new and improved habit chain for a week or so, add the final ingredient: Intense exercise. This could be as simple as doing ten pushups before taking your morning shower, or it could be something bigger, such as going for a 20 minute run to get the blood flowing and the sweat dripping.

<u>Create a Morning Habit Chain that Lifts You to Greatness</u>

By linking a few empowering habits to your morning routine, you take your mornings from chaotic, reactive, and stressful to deliberate, proactive, and empowering.

Habit Chains and Decisions

By now, you're probably familiar with the whole idea behind habit chains as well as how (and why) they work.

What we're going to do now is take deeper dive and discover *exactly* how you can exploit habit chains to help you achieve success.

Sounds pretty great, eh?

First, let's dive deeper by looking at habit chains from an entirely new angle. For most of this book, we've viewed habit chains from the perspective of them being not too dissimilar from literal iron chains. Time to toss that analogy out the window (at least for now).

So what is the very foundation of a habit chain? What is at its very core?

Let's chunk it down.

First, we have the habit chain itself. A habit chain is a collection of habits linked together into a single routine.

Let's chunk it down again. Now we're left with the individual habits that form a habit chain.

If we chunk it down once again, we now have the individual actions—actions that are repeated daily.

Chunk it down one last time and now we have this: Decisions. The decision to do something or to not do something.

What this means is that habit chains are really just a way to eliminate these decisions. When you make a habit of something, it is not longer a decision. It's just something you do. Therefore, habit chains can be viewed as a way of preplanning a collection of future decisions. This is important.

Why is this important?

You see, everybody *knows* what they need to do to be successful.

If you want to lose fat, you need to eat healthier food. If you want to earn more money, you need to increase your contribution to the world (whether by working longer, increasing your level of education, or any other way to provide more value to society). If you want to build muscle, you need to lift heavy weights and eat a healthy, protein-rich diet.

We all *know* what we need to do to achieve our goals. It's just a matter of actually *doing* those things and *continuing* to do those things.

People talk of self-discipline, focus, and work ethic as pathways to success. These are important, but there's another way: Habit. Automate the daily actions necessary to achieving what you want.

So here's what it looks like when you chunk down habit chains:

Habit chains → Individual habits → Actions → Decisions

You are your decisions. Moreover, goals are achieved by consistently making the right decisions and thus taking the right action that creates the right results that create success.

It therefore follows that you can achieve a specific goal by planning out your future decisions with a powerful habit chain.

You *know* what you need to do in order to achieve success. Now you just need to do it. By creating habit chains you can cement this and ensure that you stay on track. You chunk down the actions (i.e. decisions) that you need to make in order to achieve a desirable future and fast-track success.

If this is all sounding a little abstract, here's some relief.

So let's get this idea fleshed out a little bit. To start off, let's define it: How *exactly* do habit chains relate to decisions and how does this help you to achieve success?

First, habit chains relate to decisions because habit chains, by definition, are you basically pre-planning your actions.

Second, this helps you achieve success because you already know what you have to do to achieve success. Habit chains are just an effective way of doing what you already know you should be doing to achieve success.

Put simply:

Success is the result of making the right decisions.

Habit chains cement (and make consistent) the right decisions.

Therefore, habit chains can be used to create success.

In the above syllogism, "success" just means accomplishing a specific goal, be it losing fat, increasing your income, or anything else.

Habit Chain Decision Automation

Imagine a big machine. It has a cone-shaped mouth on top, a box-like structure in the middle, and an exit which spits out materials. It's call the HCDA (habit chain decision automation) machine.

It works like this: You decide upon a specific goal and

then chuck it into the HCDA machine. The HCDA machine then deconstructs your goal and spits out the components.

What you then do is construct a habit chain using those goal-derived components.

Here's an example: Let's say you want to better your career. This might mean making sure you get that promotion. It might mean becoming a sought-after industry expert. It might mean becoming so valuable that you're indispensable to your company.

You chuck this goal into the HCDA machine and it spits out five key components to this goal:

1. Your knowledge.
2. Your effectiveness.
3. Your value.
4. Your contribution.

Now, with the HCDA confirming that you need to better those four components, you set about creating a habit chain that will get you there.

After all, as Aristotle once wrote, "We are what we repeatedly do. Excellence, then, is not an act, but a habit." And habit chains provide an effective way to repeatedly do excellent things!

So, the habit chain you construct to consistently meet those four components necessary to reach your goal ends up looking like this:

1. Review your previous workday and write down three things you did well and three things you could improve on. *(Five minutes)*

2. Set three MITs (most important tasks) for the day. Prioritize so you don't get caught up doing busywork. *(Five minutes)*

3. Brainstorm five ways to improve your company's contribution to customers. They don't need to be good ideas, it's just an exercise to get your mind thinking about your work and industry in different ways. *(Five minutes)*

4. Read five pages of an industry-related book. Become an industry expert. *(Five minutes)*

5. Arrive at the office one hour early.

With this quick habit chain (20 minutes excluding arriving early), you dramatically increase your fulfilment of the four key components necessary to achieving your goal: Knowledge, effectiveness, value, contribution.

While this is a career-oriented goal, this exact same "HCDA machine" method can be used on any kind of specific goal you desire to achieve.

It's simple: Use habit chains to create a plan that allows you to repeat daily the activities (components) necessary to achieve success (i.e. the goal you put into the metaphorical HCDA machine).

You are your habits. Make those habit easier with empowering habit chains.

In the end, habit chains make it all that much easier to put one foot in front of the other (i.e. daily activities necessary to achieve your specific goal) when walking down the pathway to success.

Mix & Match

This "Mix & Match" section is full of lots of quick yet powerful habits. These habits can supercharge your productivity, health, wealth, and happiness.

The purpose of this section is to give you a whole list of potential habits that you can use to create a habit chain.

Of course, not every habit one could possibly form is mentioned here. This list serves only as a guide and a way to spur you on to creating your very own habit chains and achieving your own goals.

At the beginning of this book, I outlined the ideas

behind other approaches to habit formation, such as "mini habits" and "the two-minute rule." Although different from one another, they both advocate starting small.

It's easy to execute a "mini habit" or a habit that takes no longer than two to five minutes. Whether you feel like it or not, they're ridiculously easy to do. What this means is that it's much easier to do them for the 66 or so days necessary for them to become a full-fledged habit.

Accordingly, all of the habits in this "Mix & Match" section take no longer than five minutes. For each habit, I've also added a potential "mini habit" that would make it even *easier*. After all, objects in motion stay in motion—getting started is the most important thing.

Enjoy.

Habits to Supercharge Your Productivity

MITs: Every morning, write down the three MITs (most important tasks) you need to get done that day. You can also do this of an evening, planning for the next day. Identifying three MITs will not only help you focus, but it will make you more effective. *(Five minutes)*

Mini Habit: Write down the single most important thing you need to get done that day.

Improve: Write down three things (in concise dot point form) you did well that workday. Then, write down three things you could improve on from that workday. By reflecting on mistakes and/or areas where you're performing as well as you'd like to, you ensure that you're constantly growing and getting better. *(Five minutes)*

Mini Habit: Identify one thing you could do better.

Visualize: Play a movie in your mind of what your workday would look like if everything went perfectly. What would you get done? How would that meeting go? How did you eliminate distractions? And so on. Visualizing your ideal workday helps you stay on track—both consciously and subconsciously—and makes you more aware of the things that pull you away from that ideal, ultra-productive workday. *(Five minutes)*

Mini Habit: Not applicable.

Cold Shower: Rather than taking your ordinary hot morning shower, have what is called a "contrast shower." For 30–90 seconds, have the water as hot as you can (without burning yourself or having it hurt), and then turn off the hot water completely for the same duration. Repeat this once or twice, finishing with it cold. This stark temperature contrast gets the circulatory system going and the ice cold water leaves you energized and invigorated, leading to a much more productive day. Moreover, studies show that cold showers boost your immune system, boost testosterone levels, and decrease depression, among other benefits. *(Five minutes)*

Mini Habit: Switch the hot water tap off for five seconds.

Habits to Supercharge Your Health

HIIT: High-intensity interval training (HIIT) is, much like the aforementioned contrast shower habit, based on contrast. You sprint (or swim, cycle, row, etc.) as hard as you possibly can and then you jog/walk. You repeat this process for 4–5 minutes. A good ratio is 2:1. For example, you might sprint for 40 seconds and then jog/walk for 20 seconds. Studies have found that HIIT has far greater benefits than just going for an ordinary run. Other studies have also found that such exercise grows new connections in the brain and can even enable you to learn at a faster pace. Moreover, it gets the blood flowing to your brain, giving you an invigorating start to the day. *(Five minutes)*

Mini Habit: Put your jogging shoes on and walk across the street.

Fruit: Grab a piece of fruit (or even better, a vegetable!) and eat it. Yeah, that simple. *(Less than five minutes)*

Mini Habit: Peel a banana (or another piece of fruit/vegetable) and take one bite.

Sleep: One to two hours before your bedtime, go around the house and unplug your television, turn off (yes, fully turn off) your phone, tablet, laptop, desktop computer, and all other such devices. Instead, read a book, spend time with your family, journal, or do some other such activity. Not only do distracting digital devices often keep us up past our bedtime, but the blue light that they emit affects our sleep quality. A lack of quality sleep has many negative health and cognitive effects. *(Five minutes)*

Mini Habit: Turn off one digital device and hour before bed.

Habits to Supercharge Your Career

Learn: Listen to a self-help or industry-related audiobook or podcast while commuting. It takes less than five minutes a day to find relevant audio content for you to listen to while commuting. Turn your car (or bus/train) into a university on wheels! *(Less than five minutes)*

Mini Habit: Download an industry-related audiobook or podcast.

Brainstorm: Write down five ideas. They could be business ideas, ways to increase your contribution/value (and thus your income), or any other such ideas. This exercise not only lead to you striking gold every now and then, but it also sharpens your mind and makes you aware of all the options you didn't realize you had. *(Five minutes)*

Mini Habit: Think of one way you could increase the value to provide to your company or clients.

Read: Read five pages of an industry-related book or an industry journal/magazine.

Mini Habit: Read one sentence.

Grow: Try one new thing. What this one thing is depends on your job. It could be something as simple as starting a company blog or trying a Facebook ad to promote your company's product or service. If whatever you're trying is taking too long, come back to it the next day. Just make that habit of trying new things. *(Five minutes)*

Mini Habit: Think of something you could try.

Habits to Supercharge Your Happiness

Meditation: Meditation grows the brain's gray matter and helps reduce stress. *(Five minutes)*

Mini Habit: Sit on the floor, cross your legs, and take three deep breaths.

Gratitude: Write down three things you are grateful for (don't write the same three things every day). Gratitude increases your happiness and life satisfaction. *(Five minutes)*

Mini Habit: Think of one thing that made you happy recently.

Family and Friends: Give a friend or family member a quick call. *(Five minutes)*

Mini Habit: Think of a happy moment you shared with your family or friends.

Pet a Pet: Spend a few minutes petting, hugging, and talking to (if that's something you do) your cat or dog. Studies have found that petting an animal can lower blood pressure, help lessen depression, and release oxytocin (also known as "the bliss hormone"). *(Five minutes)*

Mini Habit: Look at your pet (if you have one).

Habit Chain Tips

Here are some tips to help you get the most out of your habit chains.

Habit Chain Tip #1: Keep It Short and Snappy

You're probably going to feel super motivated when you first decide to install some new habit chains and renovate your life. That's great! But there's one thing you need to be careful of: Doing too much at once. If you decide to change every aspect of your life overnight, you're going to quickly find out that you're in for quite a struggle. In fact, you'll likely end up abandoning the new habits altogether.

Fortunately, there's a simple solution: Keep your new habits short and snappy.

The best way to do this is to start off with habits that take no more than five minutes. For example, instead of signing up at some fancy gym, start with a simple health habit that takes less than five minutes—such as doing doing three sets of 10 pushups with 30 seconds rest in between.

You could also try a "mini habit."

Here's some mini habits for you to try out:

Pushup Habit: Do one pushup.
Healthy Eating Habit: Eat one piece of fruit.
Writing Habit: Write five words.
Reading Habit: Read one page.
Walking Habit: Walk across the street.

You could also try out a short and snappy habit chain.

Each habit should take no more than five minutes. Here's an example:

1. Wake up.

2. Drink a glass of water.

3. Do 10 pushups, rest for 30 seconds. Repeat three times.

4. Write down three MITs for the day.

5. Read three pages of an inspiring autobiography.

These habits take less than five minutes each, yet the results are massive. You start the day in an empowering way and build momentum that catapults you into an ultra-productive day. Even better, these habits are super easy to stick to.

Habit Chain Tip #2: Make the Chain Easy to Grip

Imagine a shiny iron chain. You grab onto the first iron ring and go to pick it up. Just as you lift it up into the air, it slips out of your hand and clangs on the floor. It's too slippery!

Habit chains are exactly the same—something I know firsthand.

A while ago, I made the mistake of attempting to create a habit chain that had a super slippery first chain. I planned on waking up each morning and immediately going for an intense 20-minute run, before going through a series of other habits.

So what happened?

Well, as you might expect, intense running isn't exactly all that appetizing when you're laying in bed beneath a pile of warm covers. Consequently, that habit chain failed to stick.

The solution?

Make sure that the beginning of the habit chain is easy to grip. Instead of going for a run immediately upon opening my eyes each morning, I instead got up, grab a cup of tea and did some easier activities such as meditating and journaling. *Then*, I went for that intense run.

The result?

Starting the habit chain was easy and so everything else naturally flowed from that.

<u>Habit Chain Tip #3: Linking and Sandwiching</u>

Although possible, starting a habit chain from scratch is difficult. If you place those habits at a random time that isn't particularly related to anything, you're going to have a hard time sticking to it.

So what's the solution?

Give your habit chains something to link onto. Alternatively, sandwich them between *two* existing habits.

For example, you might do 10 pushups before taking your morning shower. Similarly, you might think of something you're grateful for before eating dinner. You could also do some meditation or journaling after brewing your morning coffee. That's linking one habit to another.

Sandwiching works in the same way. The only difference is that you place your new desired habit between two preexisting habits rather than just linking it to one. An example might be brainstorming 10 ideas every morning between your two preexisting habits of taking a shower and brewing coffee.

Habit Chain Tip #4: Chain by Category

To determine how habit chains can be strengthened, a good idea is to examine how a real chain (e.g. iron chain) might be strengthened.

I can come up with three ideas as to how this might be

done.

First, you could have multiple iron rings linked together. This means that if one iron ring broke, there are others there to support it.

Second, you could make each iron ring thicker and stronger. This makes them less likely to break in the first place.

Third, you could make every single iron ring exactly the same. The end result would produce a much stronger chain than a chain composed of random iron rings of all different shapes and sizes.

How does this relate to habit chains? How can this help you create powerful habits that *stick*, and consequently improve your life?

Here's how: You can strengthen your habit chain(s) by composing them of similar habits.

What does this mean?

Well, take a look at two example habit chains and let me know which one you think is more likely to be adhered to and produce better results:

Habit Chain A:

1. Run.
2. Floss teeth.
3. Read.
4. Eat a piece of fruit.
5. Think of one thing you're grateful for.
6. Have a cold shower.

Or...

Habit Chain B:

1. Read.

2. Journal.

3. Brainstorm (and write down) 10 ideas.

4. Meditate.

5. Think of one thing you're grateful for.

Obviously, *Habit Chain B* is more likely to be adhered to and, for that reason, is more likely to have a positive impact on one's life.

While *Habit Chain B* consists of habits that are—in one way or another—related and easy to do one after the other, *Habit Chain A* is totally random and consists of entirely unrelated habits. *Habit Chain A* also consists of habits that would be much harder to execute consecutively.

While it is still possible to create a habit chain out of somewhat random activities, you will have a far easier time building lots of powerful habits if you categorize your habit chains. Put simply, you strengthen your habit chains by creating chains composed of similar activities.

For example, you might build a health-related habit chain to execute each morning and then a self-development related habit chain of an evening. You will yield far better results with this approach than by attempting to create a chain of unrelated habits.

Habit Chain Tip #5: Don't Break the Chain

If I wanted to destroy a suspension bridge, how could I weaken the chains that hold it up?

The answer is obvious: Cut one of the chains.

How does this apply to habit chains?

What it means is that if you suddenly decide to ditch some of the habits in your habit chain, the most likely outcome is that the whole thing will fall apart.

There are many reasons for this (such as Pavlovian conditioning and the way our brain relies on a "cue" that triggers the next habit), but it just happens.

For example, if you have a habit chain in the morning that acts as a sort of morning routine, you're likely to end up abandoning the whole thing if some of the habits that form the habit chain are skipped. If you sleep in or don't go for that run or skip that daily planning exercise (or any other habit you may be seeking to develop through the use of habit chains), you can be almost 100 percent certain that the rest of your habit chain will similarly go down the drain. Continuing the above suspension bridge analogy, the bridge will come crashing back to earth and ruin everything.

For example, I used to have a habit chain that looked like this:

1. Wake up.

2. Bodyweight workout.

3. Cold shower.

4. Banana, pawpaw, blueberry, milk, and egg smoothie.

5. Meditate.

6. Leave home.

That habit chain became my default morning routine and kicked off each day in a powerful way.

However, if I ever skipped one of the components of this habit chain (such as by skipping my bodyweight workout, having a hot shower, or sleeping in), the whole thing fell apart and the rest of my day wasn't quite as productive as it could have been otherwise.

Much like a real chain, removing a link in the chain will lead to the rest of it falling off and unceremoniously collapsing onto the ground.

Conclusion

The way to build a better life is to build better habits.

Fortunately, habit chains not only let you build better habits, but they let you build habits that stick—with less effort!

Although it sounds too good to be true, science backs you up. As discussed in the section on "The BIG 5 of Habit Chains," habit chains exploit all the inner workings of your brain—everything from Pavlovian conditioning to the science of small wins. This is why habit chains are so damn effective.

In the end, we all know what we need to do to achieve our goals. The biggest obstacle we face is consistently taking the actions necessary to achieve those goals. Habits have proven to be, and always will be, the best way to cement and make consistent positive action. The only problem is that habits can be pretty damn hard form! On average, habits require 66 days of hard effort to properly form, plus all of the self-discipline and willpower exertion necessary to overcome our current habits—the snowhill-like tracks we get stuck in.

Now you have a way around it: Habit chains.

With habit chains, you are empowered to build habits better, faster, and stronger.

And that's what habit chains are all about. Helping you retake control of your life and directing yourself toward the achievement of your biggest goals.

Printed in Great Britain
by Amazon